FOLLOWING A FAITH

A JEWISH life

Cath Senker

W

FRANKLIN WATTS

LONDON • SYDNEY

Franklin Watts
First published in Great Britain in 2018 by
The Watts Publishing Group

Credits
Series Editor: Amy Pimperton/Julia Bird
Series Designer: Krina Patel
Consultant: Elliot Steinberg, The Council for Christians and Jews

ISBN 978 1 4451 5800 6

Picture credits: Rafael Ben-Ari/Dreamstime: 20, 21t. ASAP/Alamy: 11b.
Ira Berger/Alamy: 29b. Chameleon's Eye/Shutterstock: 6, 11t, 23t. Rusian
Dashinsky/istockphoto: 9. David156/Shutterstock: 13b, 19, 32. dnaveh/
Shutterstock: 17. dpa picture alliance archive/Alamy: 22. Eterovic/Dreamstime: 26c.
Fat Jackey/Shutterstock: 12. Fotokon/Dreamstime: 8t, 31t. Eddie Gerald/Alamy:
27b. Gkuna/Dreamstime: 28. Glasshouse Images/Alamy: 10, 31b. Godong/Alamy:
2, 13t. Robert Harding PL/Alamy: front cover main. Robert Hoetink/Shutterstock:
26b. Images/Alamy: 24. Hanan Isachar/Alamy: 23b. Jeffrakespics2/Shutterstock: 8b.
a katz/Shutterstock: 29t. nadia lastovskaya/Shutterstock: front cover c, 1. Michael
Lichtenstein/Dreamstime: 25b. Arkady Mazor/shutterstock: back cover tr. Nobelus/
Shutterstock: back cover bg, 3. Richard T. Nowitz/Getty Images: 15t. David Orcea/
Shutterstock: 16bl. Guiseppe Di Paolo/Dreamstime: 27t. Jenyaolya Pavovski/
Dreamstime: 25t. Pal Pillai/AFP/Getty Images: 7. Zev Radovan/BibleLandPictures.
com/Alamy: 14, 16cr. Matthew Ragen/Dreamstime: 4. Rhonda Roth/Shutterstock:
21b. Howard Sandler/Shutterstock: back cover tl. Allen J Schaben/Los Angeles
Times via Getty Images: 15b. Alexey Stiop/Shutterstock: 5. Anastasiia Usoltceva/
Shutterstock: 18.Mingirov Yurly/Shutterstock: endpapers

The author and publishers would like to thank the following people or
organisations whose material is included in this book:
Susanna Cohen: p.7; Camila Grunberg: p.15; Rabbi Elizabeth
Tikvah Sarah: p.23; Ivan Scheer.

Franklin Watts
An imprint of
Hachette Children's Group
Part of The Watts Publishing Group
Carmelite House
50 Victoria Embankment
London EC4Y 0DZ

An Hachette UK Company
www.hachette.co.uk
www.franklinwatts.co.uk

Printed in China

MIX
Paper from
responsible sources
FSC® C104740
FSC
www.fsc.org

CONTENTS

WHAT DOES IT MEAN TO BE JEWISH?

The Jews first lived in the lands that are now Syria, Israel and Egypt nearly 4,000 years ago. They believe in one God, who made the whole world out of nothing, so everything they see, hear or experience is linked to God.

ABRAHAM AND MOSES

Jewish people believe that God made a covenant (agreement) with their ancestor Abraham to watch over them, and later revealed to the prophet Moses the laws they should follow. Therefore, Jews believe that they have a special relationship with God.

TORAH AND TANAKH

Jewish people follow the *Tanakh*. It consists of the Torah (the Five Books of Moses), plus *Nevi'im* (Prophets) and *Ketuvim* (holy writings). The Torah contains the laws that the Jews believe were revealed to Moses and show them how to live a Jewish life. The rules include the Ten Commandments, which tell people to worship one God and to respect others – for example, by never stealing or taking another person's life. The teachings of rabbis – Jewish religious teachers – help people to understand the rules.

PART OF LIFE

All Jewish people practise their faith at home and in their daily life. They go regularly to the synagogue to worship God with their community and to learn about their religion. The Jewish calendar is full of festivals, while rites of passage mark key stages in the flow of life from birth to death.

FOLLOWING JUDAISM

Although all Jews follow the Torah, there are different movements within Judaism. Orthodox Jews practise Judaism in a more traditional way. Reform Jews adapt their practices to a changing world; for instance, they accept women rabbis.

THE SHEMA

The *Shema* is the statement of the Jewish faith – the belief in one God: 'The Lord is God, the Lord is One.' Many people say it every day in Hebrew, the language of Jewish prayer.

BORN INTO THE JEWISH FAITH

Any baby born to a Jewish mother is seen as Jewish. Families bring up their children with the traditions of their faith from the start, welcoming a new baby with special customs.

BRIT MILAH

Brit milah (circumcision) is the birth ceremony for baby boys. It takes place when they are about a week old. It involves cutting off the foreskin – the skin that covers the head of the penis. The ceremony takes place in the family's home or synagogue. Brit milah is a symbol of joining the faith. The *sandek* is the man who has the important job of holding the child for the procedure. It is often the baby's grandfather. A specially trained *mohel*, usually a Jewish doctor, removes the foreskin quickly but carefully.

A SIGN

In the Torah, God gave this instruction to Abraham: 'And ye shall be circumcised in the flesh of your foreskin; and it shall be a token of a covenant between Me and you. And he that is eight days old shall be circumcised among you, every male throughout your generations.'
(Genesis 17: 10–14)

NAMING A BABY

A baby boy is given his name at his brit milah. A baby girl receives her name and is blessed by the rabbi in the synagogue, usually on the Shabbat (see pages 10–11) after her birth. Jewish parents often name a child after a family member who has passed away or a significant person from Jewish history. Many Jewish children are also given a name in the local language and a different Hebrew name, for use in synagogue rituals and prayer.

WHAT'S IN A NAME?

'We named our daughter Shira Bea which in Hebrew means 'her song within me'. Shira is named after our greatly-missed grandmother, Bea. Also, she was born when the weekly Torah reading was *Shirat-hayam* – about the Jews' escape from Egypt (see page 16). Her name combines my love for music and my husband's strong Jewish faith.'
(Susanna Cohen, Israel)

DAILY LIFE

Jewish children grow up bringing their faith into their daily life, through their dress and prayer. Most Jews follow rules about food, too.

DRESS

Boys and men may wear a head covering called a *kippah* every day; nowadays some women do too. Covering their head reminds Jews of God, the higher power above them. It is also a sign of pride in their faith. Jewish people often wear a Star of David on a chain, a symbol of Judaism.

A KOSHER KITCHEN

Jewish laws state which foods are *kosher* – acceptable to eat. Jewish people may eat the meat of animals that chew the cud (grass) and have split hooves, such as cows and sheep. To make meat kosher, the animals have to be killed in a humane way with a very sharp knife. All the blood must be removed before the meat can be eaten. Jews must also avoid eating meat and dairy products in the same meal, so these foods are stored and prepared separately from each other.

Pigs do not chew the cud and are seen as unclean, so Jewish people never eat ham or pork. Jews may consume fish that have fins and scales, but no seafood, such as shellfish, octopus or squid.

DAILY PRAYERS

Jewish people maintain their relationship with God throughout the day by offering blessings – prayers to praise him. They say blessings on waking up, before and after meals, and before going to bed. Jewish homes have a *mezuzah* in a case on their door frames (except in the bathroom and toilet). It is a tiny scroll with words from the Torah on it. When people enter the home, they touch the mezuzah and kiss their fingers. It reminds them about their faith.

PRAISING GOD

There are blessings for almost every occasion, including when experiencing wonders of nature, such as thunder and lightning. When Jews hear thunder, they recite: 'Blessed are You, God, King of the universe, for His strength and power fill the world.'

SHABBAT – THE DAY OF REST

Every week has a special day: Shabbat. According to the Torah, after making the world, God rested on the seventh day. So Shabbat is a day of rest. It starts just before sunset on Friday and lasts until darkness falls on Saturday.

GETTING READY

For Jews, preparing for Shabbat is like welcoming a very special guest into your home. Everyone helps to clean and tidy up. The Torah says Jews must not work on Shabbat, and so in Orthodox households, all the food for Shabbat is prepared beforehand. People polish the Shabbat candlesticks, put a clean white tablecloth on the dinner table and change into smart clothes.

FRIDAY NIGHT SUPPER

It is traditional to spend Friday evening at home with the family – often guests are invited too. Just before sunset, the mother lights two candles to welcome in Shabbat and says a blessing. The father blesses the children and says the *Kiddush*, a blessing over the wine, which signifies that the day is holy and special. He also blesses the *challah*, the Shabbat bread. Other adults or children can say the blessings too. Then everyone eats a fine dinner.

REFLECTION AND RELAXATION

During Shabbat, devout Jews avoid work and sports. Orthodox Jews do not drive, spend money or do housework. Writing is forbidden, so children have a break from their homework. The purpose is to focus on God and to read the Torah. On Shabbat, people can stop rushing about to relax and enjoy being with their family.

HAVDALAH

At nightfall on Saturday, Shabbat finishes with the *Havdalah* ceremony. A cup of wine is filled and blessed. Everyone sniffs sweet spices, a sign that the sweetness of Shabbat is ending. The special Havdalah candle is lit, and a blessing recited. Shabbat is over for another week.

THE SYNAGOGUE

On Saturday morning, Jewish people go to the synagogue to worship together. Orthodox Jews have to walk there. When they arrive, people wish each other *Shabbat shalom* – good Shabbat.

DRESSED FOR SHABBAT

Married women cover their hair to enter the synagogue. Boys and men (and some women) wear a kippah. Over their clothes, they wear a fringed shawl called a *tallit*. Each of the knots and strings of the fringes, called *tzitzit,* stands for one of God's rules and reminds people to follow them.

IN THE SYNAGOGUE

At the synagogue entrance is a sink where worshippers wash their hands to purify themselves before prayer. Orthodox synagogues have separate seating areas for men and women, but in Reform synagogues, everyone sits together. At the front is the Ark, where the precious Torah scrolls are stored. Above it is the *ner tamid* – the candle that is always alight, in memory of the lamp in the Jewish Temple in Jerusalem (see pages 20–21). In front of the Ark is the *bimah*, a platform where the rabbi reads the Torah.

SHABBAT SERVICE

Every week, the rabbi reads a *sedra*, a passage from the Torah. In Orthodox synagogues it is read in Hebrew, the traditional language of worship. In Reform synagogues, readings are also often made in the local language so everyone can understand. Then the rabbi talks about the meaning of the sedra – maybe relating it to life today – or speaks about a topic of interest to the community.

People recite verses from the Torah together to deepen their connection with God. Every week, the rabbi reads a portion from the Torah, until all five books have been read. Jewish people believe the Torah is the word of God, so it is treated with great respect. No one may touch the holy scrolls. The Torah is kept in a beautiful cover for protection, and it is opened and closed using rollers.

When people read from the Torah, they use a pointer called a yad.

TEFILLIN

After their Barmitzvah (see page 14), men and boys wear little leather boxes with parts of the Torah written on them called *tefillin* on their forehead and left arm for prayers. These remind them of the Ten Commandments.

13

BARMITZVAH AND BATMITZVAH

At the synagogue, the Jewish community celebrates the rites of passage through life. Young people look forward to their Barmitzvah or Batmitzvah, because it is an important occasion to mark becoming an adult in the faith.

LEARNING ABOUT JUDAISM

Boys have their Barmitzvah at 13 and girls their Batmitzvah at 12 or 13. After the ceremony, the young people become responsible for following the commandments themselves. To prepare for the event, boys and girls attend a *Cheder* – religion school – to learn about their faith. Usually they have lessons every week with the rabbi or another Jewish teacher. They discover the history, beliefs and customs of Judaism and learn to read Hebrew. The young people practise reading the portions from the Torah that they will recite at the ceremony.

THE BIG DAY

A Barmitzvah ceremony takes place at the Shabbat service on Saturday morning, and friends and relatives are invited. The boy recites from the Torah scroll and the rabbi blesses him. In Reform synagogues, the Batmitzvah ceremony is similar. For Orthodox girls, it's different. They read poetry and psalms for their Batmitzvah, but the ceremony is not part of a synagogue service.

BATMITZVAH EXPERIENCE

'My Batmitzvah preparation process provided a space for me to think about my own Jewish identity ... Although now I am officially a Batmitzvah, I will continue to consider my family history and values in my daily life.'
(Camila Grunberg, USA)

TIME TO CELEBRATE

As well as the service, friends and family are invited to a Barmitzvah party. There are several speeches, and the child thanks their parents and teachers for their support. A celebratory meal follows, with music and dancing afterwards.

PASSOVER

As well as family celebrations, there are Jewish festivals throughout the year. An important one is *Pesach* or Passover, which lasts for eight days in March or April. Passover celebrates the story of the Jews fleeing slavery.

TEN PLAGUES

The Torah tells how Jewish people living in Egypt about 3,000 years ago were forced by the pharaoh (ruler) to become slaves. They did back-breaking building work or laboured in mines. Their leader, Moses, asked the pharaoh to let them go, but he refused. God struck the Egyptians with ten horrific plagues, including lice, locusts and the death of their first-born sons.

This illustration shows Moses leading the Jews out of Egypt.

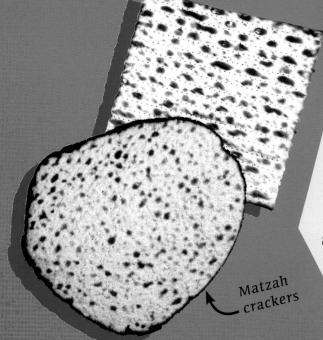

Matzah crackers

ESCAPE FROM EGYPT

Finally, the pharaoh begged the Jews to leave. Moses led them out of Egypt and through the Red Sea. With no time to bake bread, they fled carrying dough that had not yet risen. The dough went flat and hard in the heat of the Sun. To remember the tale of how God saved their ancestors, Jewish people eat crackers called matzah during Passover. They avoid *hametz* – foods made with a raising agent, including bread and cake, and any that contain grains.

THE SEDER SERVICE

On the first night of Passover, Jewish families and friends gather to read the *Hagadah*, which retells how the Jews escaped from Egypt. They eat and drink symbolic foods and wine, sing songs and enjoy a festive meal. These traditions bring the story to life for children and pass it on to the next generation.

THE SEDER PLATE

Symbolic foods linked to the Passover story are arranged on the Seder plate:

- Bone and egg – remind people of the sacrifices that were offered in the Temple (see page 20), an ancient Jewish custom
- Parsley – people dip it in salt water to remember the tears of the enslaved Jewish people
- Haroset – a sweet mixture of nuts and apples, or dates and other fruit. It is brown like the mortar the slaves used to fix bricks together
- Bitter herbs, such as horseradish – to remember this bitter time.

YOM KIPPUR

The most solemn festival in the Jewish calendar falls ten days after the Jewish New Year in September. On Yom Kippur, people think about what they have done wrong over the past year and ask God to forgive them.

Thousands of Jewish people gather at the holy Western Wall in Jerusalem (see page 26) at Passover.

SYNAGOGUE SERVICES

After the festival begins at sunset, people go to synagogue for the evening service and return the following day. The synagogues are full; even those who do not worship regularly will attend on Yom Kippur.

PRAYING FOR FORGIVENESS

The Jewish religion accepts that people make mistakes and gives them the chance to own up to them. People fast for the whole of Yom Kippur to help them to focus on God. They pray to him for forgiveness so they can make a fresh start in the new year. Fasting also helps Jewish people to think of others who go hungry, and they give to charity at this time.

The festival ends at sunset the following day. The rabbi blows a loud sound on a traditional ram's horn called the *shofar,* a symbol that people are freed of their sins. The fast is over, and people enjoy their first meal in 25 hours.

Blowing the shofar is a symbol of victory over evil and the start of a sweet new year.

BEHAVIOUR BOOKS

In the *Midrash*, which helps to explain the Torah, it is written that God has three books – the good book, the bad book and the middle book. At New Year, Jewish people believe that God weighs up how people have behaved over the past year. If they have been good, they go in the good book. If they have behaved poorly, they go in the bad book. Most people will be somewhere in the middle, and God judges them on Yom Kippur.

HANUKKAH: FESTIVAL OF LIGHT

Hanukkah celebrates a key event in Jewish history from around 300 BCE. A Greek king invaded the Jewish homeland, tried to force the Jews to worship Greek gods and wrecked the holy Temple in Jerusalem. Brave Jewish warriors called the Maccabees fought their Greek rulers and retook the city.

MIRACLE AT THE TEMPLE

When the Maccabees re-entered the Temple, they relit the ner tamid (see page 12), but there was only enough oil to fuel the candle for one day. Yet the oil lasted for eight days. To the Jewish people, it was God's miracle. To remember the miracle, Jewish people light a *hanukiah*, a candle holder with space for eight candles. On the first evening of Hanukkah, they light one candle, on the second evening, two candles, and so on for the eight days of the festival. As candlelight fills the room, they say Hanukkah blessings.

HANUKKAH SONGS AND GAMES

During the festival, people often sing Hanukkah songs and play a game with a spinner called a *dreidel*. The four Hebrew letters on its sides stand for 'A great miracle happened here' (in Israel). Foods fried in oil are eaten to remember the miracle of the oil in the Temple. Latkes are a tasty fried snack made with grated potato and onions, and jam-filled doughnuts are popular too.

PLAY THE DREIDEL GAME

Each player begins with 15 raisins, coins or other tokens. At the start of each round, everyone puts a token in the middle. If there is just one or none left in the middle of a round, they also add a token.

In turn, players spin the dreidel. If it lands on: *nun* – do nothing; *gimel* – take all the tokens; *hey* – take half of the tokens (plus one, if there is an odd number); *shin* – put a token in the middle.

If you have no tokens left, you're out. If you hold all the tokens in the game, you've won!

ACTIVE IN THE COMMUNITY

As a people who have suffered persecution in the past (see page 27), Jews are very proud of their faith. They are keen to bring people together for religious study and to celebrate their culture.

ROLE OF THE RABBI

Rabbis teach people of all ages about Jewish history and traditions and help them to learn to read Hebrew so they can understand the Torah. They lead prayers on Shabbat and at festivals, and conduct ceremonies for people at all stages of life, from birth to death. Rabbis comfort Jewish people when they are ill or sad. They also reach out to people in the wider community, for example, working with different faith groups so they can understand each other better.

Orthodox rabbis are always men, but the Reform synagogue has female rabbis too.

TZEDAKA

It is a Jewish religious duty to support the wider community by giving *tzedaka* – money to charity. People also give their own time – it's called *gemilut hassadim* (literally, acts of loving kindness). They look after sick people, take care of the children if a family is in difficulties or comfort mourners when someone has died.

HELPING REFUGEES

'As a Jewish community, it is important to help people who need support, such as refugees. In my synagogue, we have a weekly collection of toiletries and non-perishable foods for refugees in the local area.'
(Rabbi Elizabeth Tikvah Sarah, Brighton and Hove Progressive Synagogue, UK)

A religious organisation in Israel gathers food for poor Jewish families.

TIME FOR FUN

Jewish communities are very active. People come to the synagogue or community centre to take part in a variety of activities with other Jews – everything from youth organisations, parent and toddler groups and senior citizens' clubs to plays and talks on Jewish themes, traditional music and Israeli dancing.

A JEWISH WEDDING

Most Jewish people hope to meet someone special in their community to marry. A Jewish wedding celebrates the joining together of a couple and their families.

UNDER THE HUPPAH

The rabbi leads the wedding ceremony under a *huppah*, a canopy held up by four poles. It can be in a synagogue, house or outdoors. The huppah stands for the home the couple will make together. The rabbi says two blessings over a cup of wine, and the couple both drink from it. Then the groom places a ring on the bride's finger and says a blessing. The marriage contract is read out and the rabbi or family members and friends recite seven special blessings for the bride and groom.

MAZEL TOV!

It is the custom for the groom to smash a glass under his foot, a reminder of the destruction of the Jewish Temple in Jerusalem. It is a moment of sadness even at this happy time. Now the couple are married, and the guests wish them *mazel tov* – good luck. It's time for the wedding feast, followed by music and dancing.

DIVORCE

Married couples hope to stay together, but if the relationship fails, divorce is possible in Judaism. The two people apply to a Jewish court of law, and a document called a *get* is written. The husband gives it to his wife in front of two witnesses. The couple are now divorced.

PILGRIMAGE

Jewish people live all over the world. In 1948, the State of Israel was formed. It is the only Jewish state. Although pilgrimage is not seen as a duty in modern Judaism, many Jews visit Israel at least once to see the sites of important events in Jewish history, as recorded in the Torah. Some also like to travel there for a festival, such as Passover.

THE WESTERN WALL

For Jews, Jerusalem is the holiest city in Israel. It contains the Western Wall, the only remaining wall of the Second Jewish Temple which was destroyed in CE 70 and never rebuilt. Visitors touch the wall and say a prayer, or write a prayer on a slip of paper and insert it into a crevice in the wall.

TOMBS OF TORAH FIGURES

Some pilgrims visit other holy sites, including the tombs of significant figures from the Torah: Abraham, seen by many as the first Jew, and his wife Sarah; their son Isaac and his wife Rebecca; and grandson Jacob and his wife Leah. The tombs are found in Hebron.

Photos of people who died in the Holocaust at Yad Vashem.

MEMORIAL TO THE DEAD

Yad Vashem in Jerusalem is a Holocaust memorial museum to remember the terrible time during the Second World War (1939–1945) when six million Jews were killed by the Nazis. It is a sad and sombre place, but it is vital to know about this tragic history. Some people like to light candles or say prayers for those who died.

WESTERN WALL EXPERIENCE

Even those who are not devout Jews sense a spiritual feeling at the Western Wall:

'I have been a few times to the Western Wall and I am always struck by the wall's construction, size and solidity. I am not devout, but its age and what it stands for give me a feeling of awe and a sense of my connection to possible Jewish ancestors.'
(Ivan Scheer, London)

LIFE'S END

The final rites of passage bring comfort at the end of life. When Jewish people know they are dying, they ask God to forgive the bad things they have done. In their last hours, they show their devotion by reciting the Shema (see page 5).

PREPARATIONS

After the person has passed away, the body is washed and wrapped in a cotton or linen shroud (cloth for burial). A man is laid to rest with his prayer shawl (tallit). According to tradition, Jewish people are buried, although some choose to be cremated. The coffin is made from simple wood to show that in death, everyone is equal before God. A close relative remains with the coffin until the funeral.

Mount of Olives cemetery in Jerusalem, Israel.

PRAYERS

Jewish funerals are held as soon as possible after the death – usually the following day. The mourners gather at the family's home for prayers before the burial. They wear dark clothes to show respect, and men may tear a garment to show their grief.

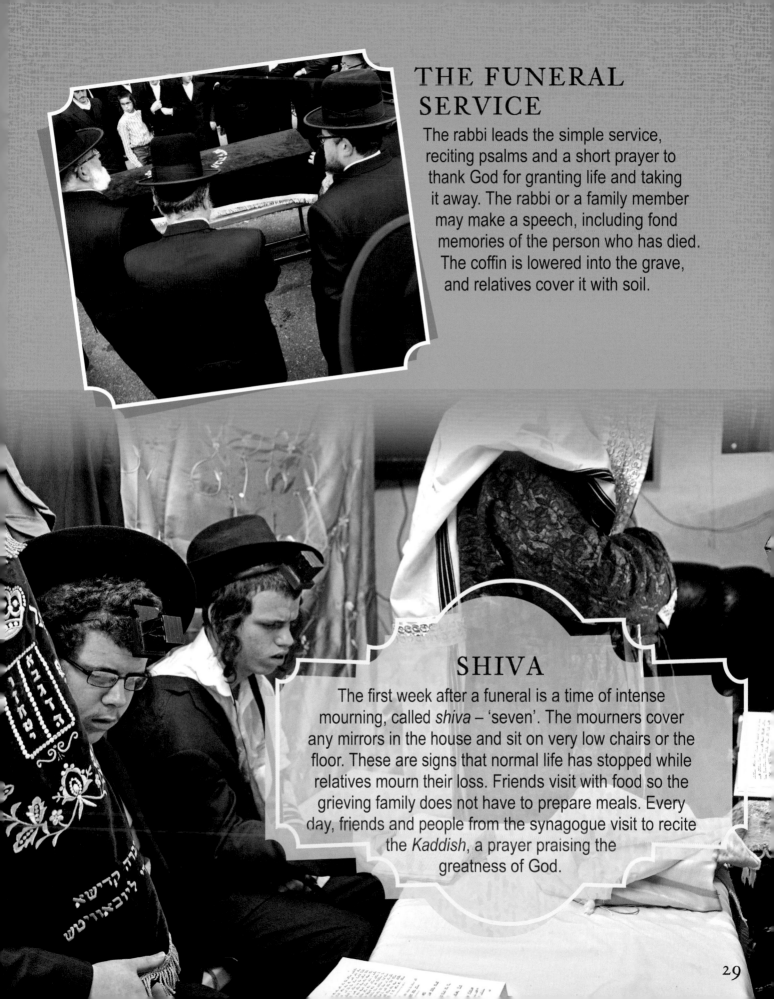

THE FUNERAL SERVICE

The rabbi leads the simple service, reciting psalms and a short prayer to thank God for granting life and taking it away. The rabbi or a family member may make a speech, including fond memories of the person who has died. The coffin is lowered into the grave, and relatives cover it with soil.

SHIVA

The first week after a funeral is a time of intense mourning, called *shiva* – 'seven'. The mourners cover any mirrors in the house and sit on very low chairs or the floor. These are signs that normal life has stopped while relatives mourn their loss. Friends visit with food so the grieving family does not have to prepare meals. Every day, friends and people from the synagogue visit to recite the *Kaddish*, a prayer praising the greatness of God.

GLOSSARY

ancestor A person in the family who lived a long time ago

Barmitzvah A ceremony and celebration for a Jewish boy who has reached the age of 13, at which he accepts the religious responsibilities of an adult

Batmitzvah A ceremony and celebration that is held for a Jewish girl at the age of 12 and 13, at which she accepts the religious responsibilities of an adult

blessing In Judaism, a short prayer for a specific occasion, often to thank God for his gifts

challah A kind of white bread that is made with egg and often plaited. Jewish people eat it on Shabbat and holidays

commandment A religious law, especially one of the Ten Commandments in the Bible

covenant An agreement. Jewish people believe that God agreed to watch over the Jewish people and in return they followed his rules

cremate To burn a dead body, as part of a funeral ceremony

fast To go without food for religious reasons

Holocaust The murder of around six million Jews by the Nazis in the 1930s and 1940s

humane Describes something done with kindness, aiming to cause as little harm or suffering as possible

Kiddush Prayer said over a glass of wine just before the meal at the start of Shabbat or a festival

kippah A small round cap worn on top of the head by Jewish men and boys, and some women

kosher Prepared according to the rules of Jewish law

lunar calendar A calendar based on the moon's cycles

matzah A large, flat cracker

memorial A statue, building or museum that is built in order to remind people of an important past event or a famous person who has died

Nazis The political party that ruled Germany from 1933 till 1945

ner tamid The candle that is always kept lit in the synagogue, as a reminder of the lamp that always burned in the Jewish Temple in ancient Jerusalem

Orthodox Jews People who closely follow the traditional beliefs and practices of Judaism

persecution Treating people badly because of their ethnic group, culture, religious or political beliefs

pilgrimage A journey to a holy place for religious reasons

prophet A person believed to have been chosen by God to spread God's word

psalm A song, poem or prayer that praises God, especially one in the Tenakh, the Jewish Bible

purify To wash to become pure in a religious sense

rabbi A Jewish religious leader and teacher

recite To say aloud

Reform Jews People who follow a form of Judaism that is adapted to modern life. For example, women play a role in worship; people may drive and cook food on Shabbat.

rite of passage A ceremony or an event that marks an important stage in somebody's life

sacrifice To kill an animal for religious reasons, as was done in ancient times in the Jewish Temple

Shabbat The Jewish day of rest, from sunset on Friday until nightfall on Saturday

spiritual To do with the mind and feelings, rather than the body, and often used to describe religious feelings

symbolic Containing symbols or being used as a symbol to stand for something

synagogue The Jewish place of worship and learning

FIND OUT MORE

Books

Celebrating Jewish Festivals by Liz Miles Hunter (Raintree, 2016)

I Belong to the Jewish Faith by Katie Dicker (Wayland, 2014)

Jewish Festivals by Honor Head (Wayland, 2012)

We are Jews by Philip Blake (Franklin Watts, 2015)

Websites

BBC Bitesize Judaism

http://www.bbc.co.uk/education/topics/znwhfg8/resources/1

Video clips about different aspects of Jewish life

BBC Religions Judaism

http://www.bbc.co.uk/religion/religions/judaism/

A good general introduction to many aspects of Judaism

Information on the Jewish religion

http://primaryhomeworkhelp.co.uk/religion/jewish.htm

Woodlands Junior School homework resources site with basic information on all aspects of Judaism

Why I like being Jewish

http://www.chabad.org/kids/article_cdo/aid/1347962/jewish/Why-I-Like-Being-Jewish.htm

Video of British Jewish children explaining their customs and festivals and why they enjoy them

Note to parents and teachers:

Every effort has been made by the Publishers to ensure that the websites in this book are suitable for children, that they are of the highest educational value, and that they contain no inappropriate or offensive material. However, because of the nature of the Internet, it is impossible to guarantee that the contents of these sites will not be altered. We strongly advise that Internet access is supervised by a responsible adult.

INDEX

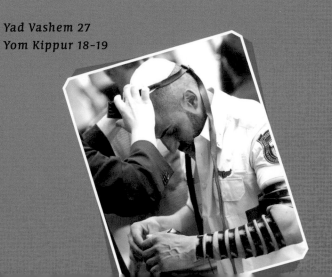

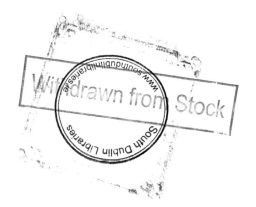